POWER PLAYS

VOLUME 6

POWER PLAYS

Drama for Worship Services and Other Gatherings

Edited by

Chuck Neighbors

A Division of Baker Book House Co
Grand Rapids, Michigan 49516

Published by Baker Books
a division of Baker Book House Company
P.O. Box 6287, Grand Rapids, MI 49516-6287

Printed in the United States of America

Library of Congress Cataloging-in-Publication Data

Power plays : drama for worship services and other gatherings / edited by Chuck Neighbors.
p. cm.
ISBN 0-8010-6793-6 (v. 1) — ISBN 0-8010-6794-4 (v. 2)
ISBN 0-8010-5045-6 (v. 3) — ISBN 0-8010-5046-4 (v. 4)
ISBN 0-8010-5235-1 (v. 5) — ISBN 0-8010-5238-6 (v. 6)
1. Drama in public worship. 2. Christian drama, American. 3. Drama in Christian education. 1. Neighbors, Chuck.
BV289 D73P68 1995
246'.7—dc20 93-38799

To Lonnie and Sue Parsons . . . your friendship is truly a gift from God. Thank you for your encouragement!

CONTENTS

ACKNOWLEDGMENTS

In addition to Celeste Pieratt, Steve Wilent, and Jim Zabloski, contributors to this book, I would also like to thank the following people for their help, support, and encouragement: Kin Millen, Marjorie Nelson, Dick Sleeper, Dan Van't Kerkhoff, the staff and drama ministry of Morning Star Community Church, Salem, Oregon, and the board of directors of Master's Image Productions. For support and encouragement on a profoundly deeper level, I thank my wife, Lorie, and my sons, Jonathan, Ryan, and Liam.

PREFACE

Who? What? Where? When? Why? The five *W*s. The inevitable questions that need to be answered by every actor seeking to develop a believable character. Two of those questions are of utmost importance: *who* and *why*—also referred to as identity and purpose.

When I am wearing my teacher/director hat, I continually emphasize the importance of these two elements. If even novice actors fully understand the identity of their characters and deliver their lines and movement on stage purposefully, chances are good that the audience will believe them. When the audience believes the characters in a play, we are well on our way to effective communication through the dramatic process. This, of course, is the goal of each drama in the *Power Plays* series.

It is my observation that the churches that use drama on a regular basis have struggled through the answers to these questions as well. The who and the why—their identity and their purpose. They have discovered or perhaps chosen an identity that includes being contemporary and/or culturally relevant. Thus, part of their purpose includes finding ways to communicate the gospel to this entertainment-crazed culture that we live in. These churches recognize that while the gospel doesn't change, our culture does; and it has done so tremendously, especially over the last fifty years.

There is no question that drama communicates to our culture. Sadly, many of the messages communicated through the current wave of movies, television, and theater are at odds with Christ's message. Because of this, some within the church are quick to condemn the medium along with the message, and that is unfortunate.

The fact is that drama is one of the most effective means of communication available. That is why so many churches are finding it a powerful tool for reaching our culture. It is more than entertainment—much, much more!

May the plays in this volume help as you communicate the identity and purpose of our Lord Jesus Christ!

INTRODUCTION

The plays in this volume have numerous possibilities. Most have been used in the context of the worship service. I like to call them "sermon setups," because they work well when presented just before a sermon. They can introduce a topic and also serve as an illustration for the pastor's theme.

The plays are open-ended, designed to raise an issue rather than answer a question, so they make great discussion starters. Use them in Sunday school classes, small-group studies, or for special emphasis programs (stewardship drives, marriage seminars, etc.).

Production Notes

- For each play, we have listed some themes at the beginning of each script. We have emphasized the more obvious themes, but after reading a play, you may discover that it would complement sermons or programs on other topics.
- For the most part, the plays feature small casts (a big advantage for most churches). While gender is specified for the characters, many of the roles can be played by members of the opposite sex with little or no modification.
- Feel free to modify the plays to fit your location by changing the names of cities, restaurants, and so forth.
- The plays can be produced as elaborately or as simply as your situation permits. Build a set if you like, or use folding chairs and a small table. If you have stage lights and/or a curtain, use them!
- If you are doing the play in the context of a worship service, do everything you can to keep the attention focused on the play. Encourage the pastor and musicians to leave the platform before the play begins, and if possible, dim the houselights.
- If you don't have a curtain or lights, we suggest ending each play in this manner: After the last line, have the actors freeze for five seconds and then exit quickly and quietly.
- Rehearse! Rehearse! Rehearse! Memorize lines! These plays are powerful and effective when done well. It would be better not to perform the play at all than to perform it poorly!

The most important production note is to encourage you to invite the Lord to be the center of every production. Pray that he will shine through each performance. After all, it is for his kingdom that you are performing!

A FISH RUNS THROUGH IT

Steve Wilent

Themes

Existence of God / Faith / Friendship

Cast

TOMMY, *of the three boys, he is the nicest*

BILLY, *he is the smartest*

MIKEY, *and he is the meanest*

Setting

A dock (a riser or bench will work).

Props

Three fishing poles, three tackle boxes, three paper bag lunches, a bag of gummy worms candy, a rubber bait worm.

The scene opens on the three young boys fishing together off the dock. All three are seated next to each other, facing the audience, and have their lines in the water.

TOMMY *(leaning over and looking down at the water)* It sure looks deep, doesn't it?

BILLY/ MIKEY *(both lean over and look, responding in unison)* Yep.

TOMMY How deep do you think it is?

BILLY Oh, I don't know. *(looking down at the water)* Maybe . . . a thousand trillion feet.

MIKEY A thousand trillion? No way.

BILLY Way!

MIKEY Not! *(looking down)* A billion maybe. But not a thousand trillion.

BILLY Okay, a billion then. *(looks down)* It's still over our heads.

MIKEY *(looking down)* For sure!

TOMMY *(looking down)* I hear that. *(pause)* My mom is going to take me to swimming lessons this summer.

MIKEY You don't know how to swim yet?

TOMMY *(defensive)* No.

MIKEY What a geek.

BILLY Leave'm alone.

MIKEY Why? He's a geek.

BILLY No, he isn't.

TOMMY *You're* a geek!

MIKEY Oh yeah? Let's jump in the water. Then we'll see who's a geek.

BILLY Knock it off, Mikey. Just because he can't swim doesn't mean he's a geek.

TOMMY Yeah!

MIKEY You don't know how to swim either, do you?

BILLY Of course I know how to swim.

MIKEY Prove it.

BILLY I don't have to.

MIKEY *(pause)* You're both geeks. *(Both Billy and Tommy turn away from Mikey and frown. After a pause he speaks again.)* You guys want to know a secret?

BILLY/ TOMMY *(in unison)* No.

MIKEY Well, I'll tell you anyway. *(pause)* I'm a geek too. I don't know how to swim yet either.

After a pause all three begin to laugh, and as they laugh they playfully slap each other on the arm. But as the laughter continues, the slaps turn to punches that increase in intensity, until finally all three are rubbing their arms in pain.

TOMMY *(leaning over the water again)* Do you guys see any fish down there?

BILLY/ MIKEY *(leaning over the water, in unison)* Nope.

TOMMY Then how do we know that they're there?

BILLY/ MIKEY *(confidently, again in unison)* They're there.

TOMMY But how do you know, if you can't see 'em?

MIKEY *(impatient)* Hey, you just know, all right? You're such a dweeb sometimes.

TOMMY I'm not a dweeb. I just don't want to waste my time. I'm a busy kid, you know. I've got homework to finish. I've got chores to do, I gotta practice my trumpet, and I gotta keep my baby sister outta my room! I can't afford to sit here all afternoon for nothing.

MIKEY You don't get it, do you, Tommy?

TOMMY Get what?

MIKEY You don't go fishing just to catch a fish.

TOMMY You don't?

MIKEY No.

TOMMY *(pause)* Then why else would you go?

MIKEY *(impatient)* To be with friends and enjoy their company, stupid. You're such a dweeb!

BILLY My dad says that you don't have to have a reason to go fishing.

TOMMY Yeah, well I do. If you want me to believe there's fish down there, you better give me a reason.

MIKEY *(irritated)* What is with you?

TOMMY Nothing! What's with you?

MIKEY Nothing!

TOMMY Fine!

MIKEY Fine! *(pause)* Any more gummy worms left?

TOMMY *(looks in a paper sack, pulls one out, and gives it to Mikey)* Yeah. Here.

Mikey pops it into his mouth without looking and suddenly starts gagging and spitting and yelling while Tommy laughs and claps his hands with glee.

BILLY What's wrong with him?

TOMMY I gave him a real worm. *(Billy laughs.)*

MIKEY *(grabbing his collar)* You want to see some fish, Tommy? I'll throw you in! Then you'll have plenty of reasons to go fishing!

TOMMY Yeah? Well if I go in *(grabs Mikey's collar)* you're comin' with me!

BILLY Would you guys chill out! Nobody's throwing anybody in the water. Besides, you deserved that, Mikey. You've been a butthead all day. (Note: If "butthead" is too strong a word for your situation, feel free to use "pain" or "jerk.")

TOMMY Yeah, a real butthead. Like my older sister. About once a month she acts just like you.

MIKEY All right, all right, I'm . . . I'm . . . sorry. *(holds out his hand to Tommy)* Friends?

TOMMY *(forgiving)* Friends.

They slap each other "five," and then each turns away, grimaces with pain, and blows on his hand.

BILLY My dad says that when he goes fishing, it makes him feel close to God.

MIKEY How does he know when God's close to him? Does he see him?

TOMMY Nobody can see God.

MIKEY Then how do you know when he's there? *(pause)* Can you smell him?

TOMMY No, you can't smell God.

BILLY You just know, that's all. Like the fish down there.

TOMMY *(laughs to himself, then makes a joke)* Sounds pretty fishy to me.

Both Billy and Mikey turn and look at him without laughing. A long silence follows.

MIKEY My uncle says that every living thing came from the ocean. *(pause)* Does that mean we all used to be fish?

BILLY I don't know.

TOMMY *(pause)* I don't think we used to be fish.

MIKEY Why not?

TOMMY Because we have to learn how to swim, bonehead!

MIKEY Oh, yeah. *(pause)* You know what Tommy?

TOMMY What?

MIKEY You're pretty smart . . . sometimes.

TOMMY *(smiling)* Thanks.

MIKEY . . . for a geek!

TOMMY *(after a moment)* Well, this is stupid. *(starts reeling in his line)*

BILLY What?

TOMMY There aren't any fish down there in that water!

BILLY How do you know?

TOMMY Because I can't see any!

BILLY Well, maybe you're not looking in the right spot.

TOMMY The right spot? Look down there! Do you see any fish?

BILLY Well, no, it's the Willamette *(or substitute local river)*! But I don't have to see 'em. I know they're there.

TOMMY *(gathering up his stuff)* I gotta practice my trumpet. See you guys tomorrow. *(Tommy exits.)*

MIKEY *(after a moment)* I'm outta here, too. *(starts reeling in his line)*

BILLY Hey, come on, Mikey! Where are you going?

MIKEY I got baseball practice pretty soon. Besides, I think Tommy's right. There's no fish down there.

BILLY Mikey, believe me, there's fish down there!

MIKEY *(not believing)* Yeah? Prove it. *(silence)* See ya. *(He gathers up his stuff and exits.)*

There is a moment of silence, then suddenly Billy's pole bends a little, and then a little more.

BILLY *(with a big grin as he works his pole)* Hello, proof!

Note: To achieve the effect of Billy catching a fish, you can attach the end of his line to something offstage. Another option is to run the line from the end of the pole back down the pole and attach it near the grip. When you reel, the pole will flex to give the illusion of a fish being caught.

GENDER GAP

Celeste Pieratt

Themes

Communication / Appreciating Differences / Marriage

Cast

PAM, *someone who likes to talk out situations before deciding on a course of action . . . as many women do*

GREG, *someone who thinks that when a situation is brought up, he is required to come up with the solution . . . as many men do*

Setting

An upper-middle class den or family room. There are an easy chair, a small desk, and a chair.

Props

Only what the director decides are needed for the particular treatment (e.g., if Greg is watching TV, you might provide cheese for him to nibble on; or if he's reading his paper, he might have a cup of coffee nearby. Pam may have just come home from work with her briefcase, which she might unpack to do some work at home.).

Greg, in the easy chair, is reading the paper and drinking a cup of coffee. Pam enters, just coming home from work. She goes to the desk and unpacks her briefcase, preparing to do some office work at home.

PAM Honey, I need to talk to you about something going on at work.

GREG Shoot.

PAM Do you remember I told you about Beth Sparks? She's the new, very ambitious senior accountant?

GREG Yeah . . .

PAM I have a feeling she's been doing a little sniping behind Mark's back, and it bothers me.

GREG What do you mean?

PAM Well, a supervisory position is coming up, and Mark's next in line for it. Beth wants it. In a lot of little ways, she's been undermining Mark's skills as an accountant and his potential as a manager.

GREG How?

PAM Little comments here and there, mainly to Howard, of course, since it'll be his decision. I'm afraid Howard doesn't see what she's doing.

GREG So tell him.

PAM He might not listen. He knows Mark and I are friends. And Beth has him completely buffaloed. She really knows how to wrap men around her finger.

GREG Do I detect a little jealousy?

PAM *(irritated)* No, you do not! This has nothing to do with jealousy. She's playing games. I can see it, Kelly can see it, Ruth can see it, every doggone woman in the place can see it. Can any of the men see it? Nooooooo. They just think she's the brightest, cutest little thing going.

GREG *(doesn't want this to go any further)* Okay. Back to your problem. Here's what you need to do—

PAM *(She cuts him off.)* What do you mean, "Here's what I need to do"? You do this to me all the time. I didn't ask for your advice.

GREG You didn't?

PAM No, I didn't. I said I wanted to talk to you about a problem.

GREG Isn't that the same thing?

PAM No, it's not.

GREG It's not?

PAM No. I can figure it out myself.

GREG *(trying to work it out)* But if you can figure it out yourself, why do you need me?

PAM I need you to listen while I work it out.

GREG *(really confused)* But if you can work it out yourself, why do you need to talk to me about it?

PAM Because it helps me.

GREG Isn't that what I was doing?

PAM No. You were trying to give me the answer.

GREG And that's not being helpful?

PAM No.

GREG I . . . I . . . I'm speechless.

PAM Now that's being helpful.

GREG What?

PAM Being speechless. You're just supposed to listen.

GREG What good's that do?

PAM It helps me to hear things said out loud, that's all. When I hear it being said, I can get it in perspective and figure out what to do.

GREG *(still confused)* But I was about to tell you what to do.

PAM I didn't ask you to tell me what to do!

GREG I . . . I . . .

PAM Oh, honestly, Greg, you're behaving just like a man.

GREG *(mock shock)* I am? Who'd have thunk it?

PAM I never have this problem with women friends. They always know that when a problem is on the table, their job is to listen.

GREG Well, when a man puts a problem on the table, he wants it solved.

PAM We want it solved too. We just don't want to be told what to do.

GREG That I can believe.

PAM Now can I go on?

GREG *(puts his paper up)* Sure.

PAM So I don't feel comfortable going to Howard because I don't think he'll trust my motivation. Peter sees what's happening, but Peter is one of those people who refuses to get involved in office politics. And he's really our strongest ally because Howard knows that about him. If Peter went to Howard, I'm sure Howard would pay attention. *(looks at Greg behind his paper)* And speaking of paying attention, will you please put that paper down?

GREG Why?

PAM So you can hear what I'm saying.

GREG I hear everything you're saying.

PAM Okay. What did I just say?

GREG You don't feel comfortable going to Howard. Peter sees what's happening and would be the logical one to go to Howard but won't involve himself in office politics. That's the summation. Do you want it verbatim?

PAM Well, put the paper down anyway.

GREG Why?

PAM So I feel like you're listening to me.

GREG I *am* listening to you.

PAM How am I supposed to know, when you're not looking at me?

GREG I can listen to you when I don't look at you. And you're just supposed to know.

PAM Oh, like I'm just supposed to know you love me even when you don't tell me?

GREG *(That came out of left field . . .)* What? *(but he sees the connection.)* Yeah, like that.

PAM Why can't you ever think like a woman?

GREG I think the answer to that is obvious.

PAM You know what I mean.

GREG Why can't you ever think like a man?

PAM What would be the point?

GREG To end discussions like this one!

PAM This is not a discussion. It's an argument. If you were a woman you'd understand that.

GREG If I were a woman we wouldn't be having this discussion.

PAM Argument.

GREG *(starts to reply, decides not to)* Can I read my paper now?

PAM What about my problem at work?

GREG I tried to tell you what to do about it.

PAM But I don't want you to—! Forget it! I'm calling Barbara. *(She heads offstage muttering.)* This always happens. This always happens. Why don't I learn? I go to him with a problem, and he tries to tell me what to do. We have a huge argument, and I end up calling Barbara to talk about it. For twenty years of marriage it's been the same thing. "Dear, I have a problem." "Dear, I have a solution." "I didn't ask for a solution." *(The ending dialogue is meant to get Pam offstage and should just be muttered to cover the exit.)*

Greg watches her go, shakes his head, then goes back to reading the paper.

MAJORITY RULES

Chuck Neighbors

Themes

Truth / Relativism / Absolutes

Cast

JUDGE BENJAMIN FICKLE, *absentminded professor type*

JAMES CAPRICE, *lawyer for the defense*

SALLY STRIKER, *prosecuting attorney*

ALICE WRIGHT, *defendant*

BAILIFF, *very official*

MESSENGER, *a walk-on, no lines*

Setting

A courtroom on the fictional Island of Cretin. Center stage are a judge's bench and the witness stand. Stage left facing right is the prosecutor's table and a chair. On stage right facing left is the defense table with two chairs.

Props

Gavel, a large, official-looking book, dictionary, file folders, and papers.

Note

This play is meant to be played broadly and for laughs. The pretext is absurd. It is in the total absurdity of the play that the point will be made. Don't be overly concerned about proper courtroom procedure. Have fun!

As the scene opens Caprice, Wright, and Striker are on stage in their proper places as the Bailiff enters.

BAILIFF *(crossing to center stage)* All rise. *(cast stands)* Hear ye, hear ye. This court is now in session. The Honorable Judge Benjamin Fickle presiding.

Judge Fickle enters and crosses to center stage behind the judge's bench and sits.

BAILIFF *(after the judge sits)* Be seated. *(moves off to the side)*

FICKLE The court calls the case of The Island of Cretin versus Alice Wright. Is the defendant present and with counsel?

CAPRICE *(stands)* She is, Your Honor. James Caprice for the defense. *(sits)*

FICKLE Is the prosecution present and ready to present its case?

STRIKER *(stands)* I am, Your Honor. Sally Striker, representing the Island of Cretin. *(sits)*

FICKLE Will the defendant please rise?

Wright and Caprice both stand.

Alice Wright, you have been charged with speaking a forbidden language. Current law prohibits speaking in any language other than English on the Island of Cretin. How do you plead?

Wright looks unsure for a moment. Caprice whispers something to Wright; then she speaks.

WRIGHT Not guilty, Your Honor.

FICKLE Very well. Be seated. *(They sit.)* Prosecution, you may present your case.

STRIKER *(standing)* Thank you, Your Honor. The prosecution would like to call the defendant, Alice Wright, to the stand.

CAPRICE *(standing)* Objection. The defendant cannot be called to testify against herself.

STRIKER Your Honor, that rule was changed. If you will refer to the Daily Law Change Log, the majority overturned that rule by a narrow margin just yesterday.

FICKLE *(looking through the book)* You're right. Overruled. Bailiff, swear in the defendant.

Caprice sits as Alice moves, nervously, to center stage and is met by the Bailiff.

BAILIFF Do you swear to tell the truth or the relative truth or the truth whatever you perceive it to be?

WRIGHT *(a bit confused)* I . . . uh . . . think so . . . I—

BAILIFF A simple "whatever" will suffice.

WRIGHT Uh . . . whatever.

BAILIFF You may be seated.

She sits, as the Bailiff moves off to the side.

FICKLE Your witness, Ms. Striker.

STRIKER Thank you, Your Honor. Ms. Wright, on the evening of Saturday, September 7, an acquaintance of a friend of a friend of yours told an unnamed source of ours that you were overheard to be speaking to a tourist on our beloved Island of Cretin.

CAPRICE *(on his feet)* Objection! Hearsay, Your Honor.

STRIKER Hearsay is now admissible evidence, Your Honor. I refer you to the Daily Law Change Log for Monday of last week. The majority voted to change the rules on last week's voting docket.

FICKLE *(checking book)* Quite right, Ms. Striker. Overruled. You may continue.

STRIKER Do you acknowledge that this conversation took place?

WRIGHT I am not sure of the date, but yes, I did speak to a tourist several weeks ago.

STRIKER Do you recall where this tourist was from, Ms. Wright?

WRIGHT Yes, he was from Hogland.

STRIKER And do you know what language they speak in Hogland, Ms. Wright.

WRIGHT They speak English.

STRIKER That is not what I understand, Ms. Wright. Our research indicates that the official language of Hogland is not English but Pig Latin!

WRIGHT Yes, but—

STRIKER Did you speak to this tourist in English or Pig Latin?

WRIGHT Well . . . Uh . . . I—

STRIKER English or Pig Latin, Ms. Wright?

WRIGHT Well, let me explain—

STRIKER Just answer the question. English or Pig Latin?

CAPRICE *(standing)* Objection, Your Honor. The prosecution is badgering the witness.

FICKLE Yes, yes. Sustained. That law has not been changed recently. I am aware that there was an effort to allow badgering in a vote last month, but the majority did not approve it.

STRIKER Your Honor, I do not perceive that I am badgering the witness. The truth, as I perceive it to be, is simply to get an answer from this reluctant witness. Your Honor will recall that we hold sacred the truth as *each person* perceives it.

FICKLE *(thinks a moment)* Why, you are quite right. Forgive me. Overruled.

CAPRICE I must object, Your Honor. The truth, as I perceive it, is that the prosecution was badgering the witness.

FICKLE Well, then, you are quite right. If you perceive that the witness is being badgered, then you are sustained.

STRIKER Your Honor, I must object. We can't both be right.

FICKLE Of course you can. The truth is and always will be relative to each person's perception of the truth—unless the law changes again. However, to settle this little dispute we will put it to a vote. Will all those in the court who think the witness is being badgered raise your hands. *(Caprice and Wright raise their hands as Fickle counts.)* One, two. All those who think the witness is not being badgered, raise your hands. *(Striker, Bailiff, and Fickle raise their hands.)*

One, two, three. Vote is three to two. The witness was not being badgered. Ms. Striker, you may continue.

STRIKER Thank you, Your Honor. Answer the question, Ms. Wright.

WRIGHT Uh, I'm sorry . . . I have forgotten the question.

STRIKER The question, Ms. Wright, was, Were you speaking to the tourist in English or Pig Latin?

WRIGHT Pig Latin. But—

STRIKER Thank you, Ms. Wright. No further questions, Your Honor. *(sits)*

FICKLE Very well. Does the defense have any questions for the witness?

CAPRICE Yes, Your Honor. *(standing)* Ms. Wright, you have testified that you did indeed speak to this tourist in Pig Latin. How is it that you know how to speak Pig Latin?

WRIGHT I was born in Hogland. My parents are Hoglandians. Pig Latin is my native tongue.

CAPRICE Can you tell the court why you were speaking in Pig Latin to this tourist?

WRIGHT He was lost. He had some trouble with formal English, so I thought I could be of help by speaking to him in his native tongue.

STRIKER *(standing)* Objection, Your Honor. The witness's motives are not relevant to this case.

CAPRICE I disagree, Your Honor. It is my intention to establish that the defendant was in the act of performing a good deed—

STRIKER I object, Your Honor. Good deeds are no longer permissible on Cretin due to the agony that they cause the majority, who suffer from the guilt inflicted by their own lack of performing same.

CAPRICE If the prosecution will allow me to finish! I am fully aware that good deeds are illegal. My intention is to establish that the defendant is a *victim* in this case. She is not responsible for her good deeds but is, rather, responding to patterns established in her childhood by parents who were fanatical in their obsession for doing good. Your Honor, I will establish that the defendant's parents were do-good-deed-aholics, so she cannot be held accountable for her actions!

FICKLE *(flipping through his book)* Mr. Caprice, I applaud your resourcefulness. That line of defense would have worked three weeks ago. However, the new laws allowing victimization of criminals as a line of defense exclude do-gooding as a valid approach. The majority simply does not want anything to do with this guilt-inducing contaminant to our society. Objection sustained! Mr. Caprice, you will please pursue another line of questioning.

CAPRICE *(sighs)* Very well, Your Honor. Ms. Wright, did you know that it was against Cretin law to speak any language other than English?

WRIGHT Yes.

CAPRICE Why, then, did you knowingly and willingly speak Pig Latin?

WRIGHT That is what I was trying to tell the court before. Pig Latin *is* English. It is just another form of the language—a jargon, if you will.

STRIKER *(standing)* I object, Your Honor. Is the defendant an expert on the English language? If not, her testimony should be considered opinion, not fact.

FICKLE Overruled. Opinion is considered fact under current Cretin law.

CAPRICE Thank you, Your Honor. However, if it please the court, I also submit that the words found in *Webster's Dictionary* also support this opinion. It reads, and I quote: "Pig Latin: A jargon that is made by systematic mutilation of English." Your Honor, as Webster points out, Pig Latin, although a mutilation, is indeed a jargon of the English language. In view of both this opinion as well as *fact,* I request that the charges be dropped against my client.

The messenger enters and carries a note to the Bailiff, who reads it silently while Fickle says his next line.

FICKLE It is fortunate for your client that this case is being tried at this time and not tomorrow. Today mutilation is legal—tomorrow it becomes illegal. Case dismissed.

BAILIFF Excuse me, Your Honor?

FICKLE Yes, what is it?

BAILIFF I have just received an urgent message about a law that will take effect immediately. I think you had better read it.

FICKLE Let me see. *(takes it from him, reads aloud)*

"In the interest of diversity, and as a gesture of understanding toward minorities, the majority has just ruled that as of twelve noon today, the new official language of Cretin will be Pig Latin. Anyone caught speaking any other language, jargon, or form of English after twelve noon today will be arrested and brought to trial."

Twelve noon. *(looks at his watch)* Good heavens—that is in five seconds.

There are expressions of disbelief as all look at their watches and wait.

FICKLE Isthay ourtcay isay ownay adjourneday. *(This court is now adjourned.)*

STRIKER But Your Honor, I object. I don't know how to speak Pig Latin.

FICKLE Ailiffbay, arrestay Izmay Ikerstray. *(Bailiff, arrest Ms. Striker.)*

Bailiff moves to arrest Striker.

STRIKER But Your Honor!

FICKLE Aketay erhay awayay! *(Take her away!)*

BAILIFF Ou'reyay underay arrestay. Omecay ithway eemay, adylay. *(You're under arrest. Come with me, lady.)*

Striker, still protesting, exits with Fickle and Bailiff.

WRIGHT Ymay, ymay. Iay eelfay orrysay orfay erhay. Aybemay Iay ouldcay elphay erhay earnlay Igpay-Atinlay. *(My, my. I feel sorry for her. Maybe I could help her learn Pig Latin.)*

CAPRICE Ownay, ownay. Onay oremay oodgay eedsday. Ellway, ouyay onway. Et'slay elebratesay! *(Now, now. No more good deeds. Well, you won. Let's celebrate!)*

WRIGHT *(exiting)* Esyay, et'slay! Anday anksthay orfay everythingay. *(Yes, let's! And thanks for everything.)*

THE PEACE OFFERING

Jim Zabloski

Themes

Parenting / Priorities / Patience

Cast

PAUL, *a father, a bit too self-absorbed at the moment*

MATTHEW, *Paul's young son*

CHRIS, *Paul's wife and Matthew's mother; not too thrilled with her husband's current lack of sensitivity*

Setting

The family's backyard with a lawn chair and perhaps some plants to give the feel of being outside.

Props

A partially assembled barbecue grill, various tools, instruction sheet, coins, glass of soda.

Paul is stooped beside a charcoal grill, tools in hand, trying to assemble it. He's frustrated at his lack of progress. Matthew enters and stands right next to him for a moment, watching, then finally speaks.

MATTHEW Whatcha doin'?

PAUL *(tightly)* Trying to build this grill. *(looks at instructions with confusion)*

MATTHEW Why?

PAUL So we can have hamburgers at home.

MATTHEW Why?

PAUL Because your mother likes to cook out.

MATTHEW Why?

PAUL *(getting tenser)* I don't know why. Matthew, give me that screwdriver over there.

MATTHEW Here you are, Daddy.

PAUL Thanks.

MATTHEW Daddy?

PAUL Yes, Matthew.

MATTHEW Cindy Edwards puked in Sunday school.

PAUL Uh-huh.

MATTHEW It was gross.

PAUL I'm sure it was, Son. *(pauses, looking at instructions again)*

MATTHEW Daddy?

PAUL *(a bit angry)* MATTHEW! *(collecting himself)* What is it, Son?

MATTHEW Can I help you?

PAUL Uh . . . yes. Yes. Would you go in the kitchen and get me . . . uh . . . uh . . . some Brillo Pads.

MATTHEW Okay. *(starts to run out, then runs back)* Daddy?

PAUL *(falls limp with frustration)* What?

MATTHEW Where are they?

PAUL Under the sink. *(Matthew runs out as his mother enters.)*

CHRIS Whoa! Where you heading in such a hurry?

MATTHEW Daddy needs some Brillo Pads. I'm helping him.

CHRIS *(approaching her husband)* Paul, what on earth do you need Brillo Pads for?

PAUL I don't. But he's driving me nuts.

CHRIS He just wants to be with you.

PAUL Well, I can't get this done, and . . . oh, never mind.

CHRIS Can I get you something to drink?

PAUL Yeah.

CHRIS What would you like?

PAUL Anything. Cola, lemonade. I don't care.

CHRIS We don't have cola or lemonade.

PAUL *(getting frustrated with her, too)* Anything, Chris! I don't care. Whatever we've got. Surprise me.

CHRIS *(A bit upset with him for getting angry with her, her response hints of an "I'll get you, buddy" tone.)* You got it. *(prepares to exit when interrupted by Matthew running up to them)*

MATTHEW Daddy?

PAUL What?

MATTHEW What are Brillo Pads?

PAUL *(in desperation)* CHRIS! PLEASE!

CHRIS Come on, Matt. Help Mommy for a few minutes in the kitchen.

MATTHEW But Daddy needs me to help him.

PAUL Matthew, I don't need you! Now go help your mother!

Matthew exits, dejected.

CHRIS Paul Reiley, there is no need for you to snap at him like that! I don't want that stupid grill if you're going to act like that. Why don't you just take a few minutes break and get away from it and cool off? *(She exits.)*

He puts his tools down and flops in the chair, mumbling to himself. Gets back up, grabs the instructions, and sits down again to ponder them. Goes back to the grill and begins to tinker again. Matthew enters, his hands clenched on something, and stands by Paul.

MATTHEW Daddy?

PAUL Yes. *(doesn't look up)*

MATTHEW *(long pause)* Daddy?

Chris enters carrying a glass of soda, but stands at a distance to listen.

PAUL *(sighs, but keeps working)*

MATTHEW Daddy?

PAUL *(drops his tool, grabs Matthew by both shoulders and angrily says)* WHAT, MATTHEW? WHAT NOW?

MATTHEW Mommy said you wanted some lemonade. So I took the money out of my Barney bank, and I wanted to buy you some, and I thought you would go with me so I could buy you some, and . . . and . . .

Matthew drops his head to cry. Paul's heart is broken at Matthew's words, and he pulls him tightly to himself in an embrace.

PAUL Oh, Matthew, Matthew. I'm sorry. Daddy's sorry. *(Chris in the background wipes her eyes, as the lights fade.)*

AIRPAIN

Steve Wilent

Themes

Dealing with Fear / Faith / Hypocrisy

Cast

GATE AGENT, *polite and cheerful*

DR. BOB, *a psychologist, nurturing and patient*

FRANCINE, *overly emotional and excitable*

RICK, *negative, sarcastic, and cynical*

CHARLES, *nerdy, nervous, and easily influenced*

Setting

The airline terminal boarding area for Chance Airlines. Four chairs (or a long bench) face the audience center stage. There is a check-in counter stage right.

Props

A sign saying "CHANCE AIRLINES," a microphone, three plane tickets, a purse, a small container of milk, and one large cookie.

As the lights come up, we hear a jet fly overhead and see the boarding area for Chance Airlines. The gate agent stands behind the counter, microphone in hand.

AGENT Your attention, please. Chance Airlines flight 13 to Bermuda is now boarding. Carry-on bags, parachutes, and rabbits' feet may be stored in the overhead compartments. For your convenience, Chance Airlines provides a preflight courtesy service including personalized life insurance and last will and testament preparation. Please remember that all Chance Airlines flights are smoking flights, because really—what's it going to matter? Thank you for flying Chance and taking a big one with us.

Agent exits as four people enter from stage left. In the lead is Dr. Bob, and following him nervously are three others who walk in single file like small children at a crosswalk.

DR. BOB All right, everyone. We're here. Let me give you your tickets. *(He hands them out.)*

FRANCINE *(holding up her ticket)* Oh, this is so invigorating! I feel like I've just been handed my diploma.

RICK *(cynical)* Don't count your engines before they fall off, Francine.

CHARLES *(nervous)* Yeah, we're not even on the plane yet.

FRANCINE *(indignant)* Dr. Bob, I don't think Charles and Rick are quite up to this, do you?

DR. BOB They'll do just fine, Francine. Trust me.

FRANCINE Well, among the three of us I seem to be the only one expressing a positive attitude. You said that the first step in overcoming one's fear of flying is nurturing a positive attitude.

RICK *(sarcastic)* Oh, I have a positive attitude, Francine. I am absolutely positive that we're all going to die.

CHARLES *(walking away scared)* I'm outta here!

DR. BOB Rick, tell Charles you were just kidding.

RICK I was just kidding, Charles.

CHARLES *(stopping)* Oh. *(He walks back with a change of attitude.)* I'm back.

DR. BOB Now, before we board the plane, let's rehearse the takeoff one more time. *(All four sit in the seats facing the audience.)* First, we buckle our seat belts, making sure that they are snug *(They mime the action, pulling too hard while sucking in their stomachs.)* . . . but not *too* snug. *(They loosen them slightly with sighs.)* Next, we check our breathing, making sure that it is slow and even. *(Everyone exhales slowly while saying the word "slow." Then everyone inhales slowly while saying the words "and even." They repeat this twice.)* Now as the plane slowly taxis onto the runway, we begin our Emotional Imagery Techniques. Francine . . .

FRANCINE *(as if in a trance)* I'm lying in a hot bath. A gentle breeze carries the scent of chamomile and hibiscus past my nostrils. I am calm. I am cared for. I am content.

DR. BOB Charles . . .

CHARLES *(same trance)* I am six years old. I am sitting at the kitchen table. Mummy brings me a plate of chocolate chip cookies and a frothy glass of whole milk. I am calm. I am cared for. I am content.

DR. BOB Rick . . .

RICK *(same trance)* I've just downed a tall one at Pete's Sports Bar. On the big screen, I'm watching the Blazers win the NBA championship. Suddenly, my ex-wife walks in and informs me that she has just been chosen to be the first female astronaut to permanently inhabit the planet Mars. I am calm. I am cared for. I am content.

DR. BOB Good. You're all doing very well.

FRANCINE Dr. Bob?

DR. BOB Yes, Francine?

FRANCINE What about *your* E.I.T.?

DR. BOB My E.I.T.?

CHARLES Your Emotional Imagery Technique.

DR. BOB Oh. Ahh, there's not enough time for mine. *(changing the subject back)* Okay, now, you're all calm, you're focused, you're breathing evenly . . . the plane slowly begins to pick up speed as it moves down the runway . . . faster . . . and faster

. . . and faster . . . the nose of the plane begins to rise . . . there's a slight pressure against your chest . . . *(They all react to the pressure too strongly.)* . . . I said a *slight* pressure. *(They do it again correctly.)* Good. Then suddenly, as you feel the rear wheels leave the ground . . . you're airborne!

CHARLES *(screaming with fear)* Aaaaahhhhhhhhhh!!!

DR. BOB *(moving over to him)* Charles! Charles, calm down! You're fine. You're fine. You're all right. *(Charles is not convinced.)*

FRANCINE *(dutifully taking a cookie and small container of milk from her purse and handing it to the doctor)* Cookies and milk, doctor?

DR. BOB *(taking it)* Thank you. *(He takes a bite and a sip.)*

FRANCINE Doctor.

DR. BOB Yes?

FRANCINE Those are for Charles.

DR. BOB Oh. Oh, yes. Of course. Here, Charles. *(hands them to him)*

CHARLES *(after a bite and a sip)* I feel better now. Thank you. Oh, Dr. Bob, what is wrong with my faith? Why, after months and months of counseling, do I still have doubts? Why am I so afraid to fly?

RICK *(interrupting)* Because you're a wimp.

CHARLES Oh, yeah, well, I don't see you champing at the bit to get on board!

DR. BOB Fellas, fellas, please. Let's settle down here. Charles, there's nothing wrong with having doubt. That's okay. What we need to do is work through those doubts by reviewing the facts. Now, let's review Dr. Bob's Five Facts of Fearless Flying, shall we? Number one: What is statistically the safest form of travel known to man?

ALL Flying.

DR. BOB Number two: What company was secretly responsible for the movie *Airport* and all of its sequels?

ALL Amtrak.

DR. BOB Number three: If there was an earthquake, where would you be the safest?

ALL In the air.

DR. BOB Number four: What mode of travel does the president of the United States use the most?

ALL Flying.

DR. BOB Number five: Can we trust the president?

ALL *(start to answer but suddenly stop and look at each other in doubt)* Uhhhhhhh????

DR. BOB Yes. The answer is yes. Here, read my lips, yes.

ALL Ahhhhhh . . . yes.

DR. BOB Good.

AGENT *(Agent enters during last bit of dialog and goes to microphone.)* Your attention, please. This is the last call for Chance Airlines flight 13 to Bermuda. Please board immediately. Thank you.

DR. BOB Well, off we go! You're all going to do just fine, I'm sure of it!

They pick up their bags and head toward the gate, stage right. Dr. Bob lags behind, near the ticket counter. Amid ad-libs of excitement and positive thinking about their flight, the three, after handing their tickets to the agent, exit, leaving Dr. Bob at the gate.

AGENT Your ticket, sir?

DR. BOB Ticket? Oh, I'm not going with them.

AGENT Why not?

DR. BOB You gotta be kidding! I'm an important psychologist. Many people depend on me for their sanity. I can't go around risking my life in one of those flying coffins!

LOOKING BACK, LOOKING ON

Jim Zabloski

Themes

Denial / Healing the Past / Courage

Cast

CANDICE, *a thirtysomething, beautiful, talkative, and somewhat uncaring older sister; in denial about her past*

MARY, *the younger sister, a bit plain and less confident*

Setting

We are in Candice's bedroom. There are a chair, an easy chair, and a makeup stand with a mirror. The room should look opulent.

Props

Makeup, purse, two beverage glasses.

Note

Southern accents might add a nice touch to these characters.

CANDICE *(hears distant knocking on door, is busy applying makeup, answers in a singsong fashion)* Come in. *(louder)* COME IN. *(Enter Mary, standing at the doorway holding a purse. Candice sees her and continues as before.)* Oh, Mary. This is a surprise. Go ahead and sit down in the living room. Get yourself something to drink or whatever. I'll be out as soon as I finish putting on my makeup. Please don't pay any attention to this messy bedroom. I usually make my bed, you know, but today has just been a tornado, just a tornado. *(Mary remains stone still. Candice notices.)* Mary, is everything all right? I said I'd be with you in a minute. Now why don't you be a sweetheart and fetch us both something to drink? *(Mary drops her purse, exits to the kitchen and returns with two glasses. She stands next to Candice holding them while Candice continues applying makeup.)* Well, darling, don't just stand there like a statue. Set them down. *(Mary sets one on the makeup stand and sits holding hers.)*

MARY Candice?

CANDICE Um-hmmm?

MARY Do you ever think about Daddy?

CANDICE Um. Oh, all the time. All the time.

MARY He's been gone twelve years now, you know.

CANDICE Has it been that long? My!

MARY I've been thinking about him a lot lately.

CANDICE *(stops)* Oh, now, don't tell me you're going to get all blubbery on me. I couldn't stand it.

MARY No, I'm not going to "get blubbery." It's just that . . . well . . . well, you know I've been going for counseling.

CANDICE Oh, yes, the headshrinker. What's his name? Dr. Graceman?

MARY Classman . . . Dr. Classman. And he's not a headshrinker, Candice. He's been very helpful and kind and—

CANDICE Well, I'm sure he's done a world of good for you. Although, I can't for the life of me figure out what on earth you need a shrink for.

MARY *(irritated)* He's not a shrink, Candice. He's a counselor. I just had some things I had to work through, that's all, and he's helped me find myself. Helped me find some things out. That's all.

CANDICE Well, darling, you never were very good at showing your feelings. I can remember as a teenager you were so quiet. How you ever kept yourself so calm all those years when all the other girls your age were so wild! Including me.

MARY That's what I've come here to talk about.

CANDICE What? Your teenage years? Oh, please! Let's leave the past in the past, shall we? No need in dragging it all up again. You lived it once, why on earth would you want to relive it?

MARY Dr. Classman was right. You are in denial.

CANDICE *(turns angrily)* You've been talking to that shrink about me behind my back?! How dare you?

MARY Look, Candice, I did not drive all the way over here to fight with you again. I came over here to help myself, to help you . . . to help both of us.

CANDICE Well, I don't need any help, thank YOU!

MARY Yes, yes, you do, Candice. And the fact that you can't see that you need help ought to tell how much you do need it.

CANDICE I have a date. I don't have time for this. Now, if you'll excuse me—*(crosses to door)*

MARY Daddy hurt you too, didn't he?

CANDICE What?

MARY He hurt you. He hurt you first, and when he was through with you, he came to me.

CANDICE Mary, what on *earth* did that lunatic doctor put into your head? What *are* you talking about? Daddy? Hurt me? I was his favorite little girl, and we both know it. You've always been jealous.

MARY You can't run away from it forever, Candice. Sooner or later it will catch up to you like it did me. The longer you run and hide from the past, the bigger the monster grows.

CANDICE That's pretty smart talk for a C student.

MARY *(ignoring the comment)* I used to pretend I didn't hear it. When he was done, I'd lay in bed waiting for you to come talk to me, but you never did. You kept it all hidden inside, like you're doing now. You thought I didn't know? I knew.

CANDICE He didn't. *(weakening)*

MARY You'd cry till you fell asleep. I heard you. Then I'd fall asleep and wake to another nightmare, night after night, day after day.

CANDICE *(more broken)* This is all in your head.

MARY It took me two years to face it myself, and another six months to face you. Candice, we are two broken women in need of repair. The reason I came here . . . *(approaches her to hold her)* the only reason I came here tonight was to help you. I don't want to hurt you. I never wanted to hurt you. I needed you as much as you needed me . . . as much as we need each other now. Candice, I'm reaching out to you as your sister and friend. Please, let's talk about this.

CANDICE *(long pause as Mary holds Candice, who finally gathers herself together, breaks away, and sashays around the room, walks over to the makeup mirror for one last look, then faces Mary)* I feel sorry for you, Mary Elizabeth, I really do. But if you want to live in a . . . a wild fantasy world, then you go right ahead. I prefer to live my life in the here and now. *(walks toward the exit)* You're welcome to stay as long as you like, just clean up after yourself before you leave. Please help yourself to whatever's in the refrigerator and lock the door on your way out. Now, I have a date. *(a few more steps to the exit, then turns with one more thought)* Watch yourself going home. A girl's got to learn to protect herself. *(She exits.)*

THE COOKIE CONNECTION

Celeste Pieratt

Themes

Temptation / Friendship / Self-discipline

Cast

JANE, *a young woman who has just managed to lose forty pounds*

SANDY, *a friend of Jane's; supportive and perceptive*

LILLIAN, *also a friend; would like to be supportive but . . .*

Setting

A kitchen or combination kitchen/dining area, with a table and three chairs.

Props

Coffee and cups (or iced tea pitcher and iced tea, whatever the preference), a cake cut up into small pieces, a plate of cookies, a bowl of fruit.

As the scene opens, Sandy is seated at the table. She may be reading a magazine or studying for college exams. A beat, then Lillian enters with Jane in tow.

LILLIAN Sandy, look who dropped by for a cup of coffee.

SANDY *(goes to her and gives her a hug)* Jane, it's so good to see you. It's been months! *(stands back and surveys Jane)* You look wonderful. How many pounds did you lose?

JANE Forty. I feel marvelous.

LILLIAN Doesn't she look great? What plan were you on?

JANE Marla Stevens. *(seeing all the baked goods)* Who's been doing baking?

LILLIAN Me. The church was having a bake sale, but I never got around to taking them. Want to help us finish it all off?

JANE *(weak laugh)* I don't know if I should be here surrounded by all this.

SANDY We'll help you be strong. So what about this diet? *(As they are talking, Lillian is busy getting coffee.)*

JANE It's one of the prepared-foods diets. I am so glad to be off it. The food was fine at the beginning, but boy, did it get old after awhile.

SANDY Some of those types of plans don't teach you how to eat healthfully afterward. Did this plan?

JANE They offered seminars, but I don't need them. I'm in control now. I'm never going to revert to a size 16 again.

LILLIAN You look wonderful. *(shoves a piece of cake at her with the coffee)* Here. Have some cake with your coffee.

JANE I'd better not.

LILLIAN Come on, you can afford it now.

JANE Lillian, if I start I won't stop. Trust me on this one.

LILLIAN You said you were in control. You can have just one teeny piece.

SANDY Lillian, leave her alone. Have you changed your eating habits?

JANE Not really, but I know what I need to stay away from. My downfall has always been sweets. I'll just make sure I don't keep any around the house. That way I won't be tempted.

SANDY Did they at least help you identify when you were most likely to slip and help you find a substitute?

JANE They had counseling available for that, but honestly, Sandy, I didn't feel I needed it. I just refuse to let myself get depressed any more.

LILLIAN *(shoves a plate of cookies toward her)* Good for you. Here, have a cookie. They're small.

JANE *(a groan)* Butter cookies. *(They're her favorites, but she's going to be strong.)* But I can't.

LILLIAN I have to brag, Jane. They're the best batch of butter cookies I ever baked.

JANE I'm sure they are.

LILLIAN Just one.

SANDY Lillian, will you stop?

JANE *(to change the subject)* What's happening at work?

LILLIAN *(While Lillian talks and until more action is dictated, Jane eyes the cookies, the cake, or both. At some point she'll almost start to take one, but Sandy either lightly slaps her hand or moves the cookies away.)* We're getting new word processing software, but Inga positively insists on getting Word Fab. I keep trying to tell her that Wonder Word is a much better program for us, but she won't listen. Word Fab has a better marketing department, and that's all it has going for it. Oh, I guess it's superior for legal work, but we also do medical transcription and financial statements. Wonder Word's not as good for legal, but Word Fab is much worse for financials and doesn't come with a medical dictionary. So anyway, I've been trying to convince Inga, but the Word Fab salesman has her convinced it's the best. Sure you won't have a cookie?

JANE *(shakes her head)* How's Martin?

LILLIAN Fine. He's up for a promotion at work. I'm hoping . . .

JANE Yes?

LILLIAN Well, I don't want to count my chickens, but I think once he gets it, he'll pop the question.

JANE *(Not so wonderful. Lillian's good fortune makes her think of her recent breakup.)* Wonderful.

SANDY Speaking of men, what happened with Hal?

JANE *(shrugs)* We broke up. *(tries to be brave, but it doesn't last long)* But it's better. I'm ready for a commitment and he's not. We were at different places in our lives and had grown apart. I'll be happier without him . . . eventually . . . but . . . I miss him. I really miss him. *(From here on, Jane should get more and more depressed with her situation, a little weepy and whiny. But it should be kept light. This is not a tragedy.)*

LILLIAN I know, dear. *(She pushes cookies toward Jane. Sandy pushes them away.)* But it's better that you broke it off now. I never liked him for you anyway. Any man who would wear blue pants with brown socks can't have a clue about women. *(She shoves the cake at Jane. Sandy shoves it away.)*

JANE I've been trying to bury myself in work, but that's not working either. Course I don't know if that's the best idea. I'd just be prolonging the mourning period, and it would sneak up on me later. Maybe I will have a cookie.

SANDY *(pushes the fruit toward Jane)* Have some fruit instead.

LILLIAN How's Vanessa doing? You know, of all the people we used to work with I admired her most, I think. She was so conscientious and so capable. She knew that office inside and out—where to go to find what and who to handle it most efficiently.

JANE She was laid off. *(short laugh)* That's why I can't bury myself in work. There's not enough of it. They're downsizing. *(wails)* I may lose my job. *(small sniff)* What kind of cake is that?

SANDY *(shoves the grapes over)* Grape.

LILLIAN Oh, no. Jane, I'm so sorry. Uh . . . how are your parents?

JANE Moving. They're moving to Phoenix at the end of the month. My mother and father are leaving me! *(to Sandy, mournfully)* Why can't I have a cookie?

SANDY Size 16 . . .

LILLIAN But you and your parents are so close!

JANE I know, but they're sick of the earthquakes *(tornadoes, hurricanes, whatever the local natural disaster is).*

LILLIAN *(trying to find a safe, happy subject)* Your roommate?

JANE *(wails)* She's getting married! She can find a husband and I can't and now I have to find another roommate.

LILLIAN *(doesn't know what else to do or say)* Cake?

JANE *(wails)* Yes! *(starts to grab for it; Sandy puts a banana in her hand instead)*

SANDY I'm not going to let you, Jane.

JANE Please, please, please, just one piece of cake. Just one teeny little piece.

SANDY You won't stop there and you know it. Jane, you did too much hard work to lose that forty pounds, and I'm not going to let you slip back into your old habits. Eat the fruit!

JANE *(sniffing, takes the fruit)* Thank you. I hate you, but thank you. *(takes a bite of the banana and looks at it as though it were sour)* I think I'll go home now. I'll come back another time.

LILLIAN You're leaving so soon?

JANE Yes. I won't be good company anymore. *(takes another bite of the banana, makes another face, exits)*

SANDY/ LILLIAN *(overlapping)* Bye, Jane. Take care. Bye-bye.

SANDY *(Sandy starts to clean up, then suddenly remembers something.)* Isn't there a Baskin-Robbins between our place and hers?

LILLIAN And a Mrs. Fields.

SANDY Jane, wait! I'm following you home! And we're stopping at the Fruit Mart!

She exits, leaving Lillian onstage. Lillian shrugs and takes a cookie.

THE LETTER

Chuck Neighbors

Themes
Suicide / Grieving / Forgiving Self

Cast
NEIL, *a father trying to cope with a terrible loss*

Props
Notepad, pen, chair, desk.

Note
This play deals with the suicide of a teenager. If played properly, the audience should not figure out that the son being written to is dead until the end of the play. This makes the impact of the play even stronger. While the play is emotional, the actor playing Neil needs to use restraint in his emotions until the end so as not to foreshadow the ending.

Though the actor "reads" the letter, it is important that he not focus just on the letter. His eyes need to come off the page as he reflects, thus letting the audience in on his thoughts.

As the scene opens we see Neil onstage behind the desk. He is just finishing a letter. He looks it over, nods slowly in approval, and begins to speak.

NEIL *(to himself)* There. It's done. *(a pause, then he starts reading the letter)*

Dear Son,

It's your birthday today, and I felt a need to write you this letter. It has taken a long time for me to be able to answer your letter. So much has happened lately that I want to share with you. I wish you were here so we could share in person.

Your mother is doing very well. This last year has, of course, been a struggle—not having you around. Yesterday we went shopping. You know your mother and shopping—she shops and I warm the bench outside the store. We passed by a computer store, and naturally, I started thinking of you. In fact, I considered buying you this new game, then I remembered. Oh well, probably would have been obsolete before I got it home . . . things change so fast these days.

Anyway, what I want to tell you is that I have made what I feel is an important discovery. You see, I have come to understand that I have really failed you as a father. I have always loved you but had a hard time showing it, let alone saying it. My way of showing it was to give you the freedom to do whatever you wanted, even when you were very young. I was always, as they say, permissive with you, even when I *wanted* to say no. I was afraid that I would somehow lose your love. I mistakenly thought that if I said yes to everything, you would love me back. I gave you everything you asked for, hoping for your love in return.

Part of my reasoning was out of rebellion toward my own parents. They were so strict, and I vowed never to be like them. Instead of finding a happy medium, your mom and I went to the other extreme. Now I see how wrong that was. Our permissiveness was interpreted by you as not caring. Even though we didn't approve of the crowd you chose as friends, the parties, and as we found out later, the drugs—it took us a long time to come to grips with that one—we chose not to intervene. But I did care; I was just afraid. Afraid I would drive you away. In the end I did just that.

But I have to tell you, Mom and I have learned a lot lately. We are in counseling and have even started going to church. I know, I know, we used to go when you were very young but stopped when you complained . . . our mistake again. Anyway, we *are* going now, and I am learning more about being a father as I learn more about God, our heavenly Father. I realize now, more clearly, the mistakes I made with you. Mom and I have become Christians and . . . I know you probably won't believe it . . . but it has made a big difference in our lives.

I guess what I want to say—need to say, really—in response to your letter, is that we don't blame you, at least not totally, for what you did. We have to share in the blame. It has taken a long time for me to come to grips with all that has happened, but through Christ I have found forgiveness. I have also forgiven you for your part. I only wish I could have yours. I guess it is too late for that.

It saddens me that you will never read this letter, but somehow it has helped me to write it just the same. Happy birthday, Son.

I love you.

Dad

He thinks a minute, then begins to write again.

P.S.: Mom and I bought flowers for your grave today. I wanted to get that computer game, but Mom insisted . . . *(breaking down in tears)* Maybe next year.

No stranger to the stage, **Celeste Pieratt** has been involved in theater for more than twenty-six years. As an actress and director she has toured in professional repertory theater throughout the United States, Canada, and Australia. Celeste, part of the writing team for Master's Image Productions, wrote Chuck Neighbors' one-man show on drug and alcohol abuse, *Scenes Unseen,* and co-wrote his one-man show, *Pillars*. Celeste is the director of the drama ministry for St. Stephen Presbyterian Church in Chatsworth, California.

Steve Wilent is the drama director of South Hills Community Church in Portland, Oregon. He has eighteen years of practical experience in the field of drama and has been involved in more than three hundred productions, writing more than half of these. In 1980 Steve left a promising acting career in Hollywood to attend Bible college and seminary. He is a former pastor. He and his wife, Ila, have two children, Melissa and Jameson.

Jim Zabloski has been involved in drama for over twenty years, performing in traveling children's theater, high school productions, and civic theaters. He has authored numerous sketches for church drama ministry and is on the programming team at First Baptist Church of West Hollywood, Florida. Jim has also written over one hundred songs as well as an Easter musical. He and his wife, Linda, and their two sons currently live in Fort Lauderdale, Florida.

In addition to performing several one-man dramas,
Chuck Neighbors also conducts workshops for churches
that would like to develop their own drama ministry.
For information write to:

Master's Image Productions
P.O. Box 903
Salem, OR 97308